The Safari Series

Ally the Aardvark and the Shy Five

Story by Ian Pletzer

Illustrations by Joni-Leigh Doran

Editing by Narina Exelby. Internal book design and cover design by Joni-Leigh Doran.

This book is dedicated to the future conservationists of the world.

Ally is an aardvark. Most people have never heard of the aardvark, and many of those who have, know it only as the first word in the English dictionary. The word "aardvark" actually comes from the Afrikaans language. Meet the "earth pig"!

Aardvarks are very shy, solitary creatures – so shy, in fact, that people don't see them very often, if at all. They are nocturnal, which means they are active mostly at night. It is because of this that aardvarks form part of a special group of animals called the "Shy Five".

Ally has big, big ears, an even bigger nose, and the biggest tail ever! She used to worry that people would think she looks a bit odd, and this made her feel shy, so she rather liked to stay hidden away. During the day she spent all of her time deep underground in a burrow that she had dug by herself. Aardvarks dig lots of big, deep holes in their search for termites and ants.

They also like to sleep deep inside these burrows.

Pip the porcupine is also one of the Shy Five, and he also lives in one of the burrows dug by Ally. Just like Ally, Pip is nocturnal, and occasionally the two of them have a brief chat on a moonlit night before they scuttle off to find their different dinners.

(Pip isn't really into termites and ants. He's a vegetarian and prefers to eat fruits, roots, tubers, bulbs and bark.)

Sometimes Ally passes another of her shy friends, Arnold the aardwolf (which is also an Afrikaans word, meaning "earth wolf"). Arnold's favourite meal happens to be termites too, but he loves all insects. He uses his large ears to listen out for these delicious delicacies.

Arnold is also extremely shy... even shyer than Ally. Some would say that Arnold is the shyest of the Shy Five.

One winter during a particularly long, icy snap of chilly weather, it was too cold for Ally to leave her burrow at night – the temperature was f-f-f-freezing! You need to remember that Ally is a big girl; she needs lots of termites and ants to fill her up and so after hiding underground in her burrow and skipping dinner for a few cold nights in a row, she was very, very hungry indeed. Ally really needed to eat!

The next day, Ally broke her rules. Her hunger pains were so severe that she forgot she was shy and she left her safe burrow in broad daylight in search of food.

Max the meerkat was out with his family. Max was on lookout duty, standing on his hind legs, scanning the sky and the horizon for predators. He is the least shy of the Shy Five, and probably the most famous. Max was surprised to see Ally out in the day. “Hey Ally, what are you doing out here?” he asked. Ally replied, “I’m so hungry! I need to find something to eat.”

Max had a look around and told her that the coast was clear.

Ally passed Bob the bat-eared fox, another member of the Shy Five who also happened to be out in the sunshine. Bob has big ears like a bat and he was using them to listen for any creepy crawly bugs he could snack on. Bob also seemed surprised to see Ally, but he had bigger fish to fry – or rather, bugs to bite.

Ally started using her great big nose to sniff out the termites. Sniff, sniff, sniff.

She also used her enormous ears to listen for termites. Listen, listen, listen...

Dig! Dig! Dig! Ally used her large claws to scratch the dirt and her long sticky tongue to slurp up the insects. Yum, yum – food!

Ally was so busy feeding on termites that she didn't see a safari vehicle getting closer and closer.

Suddenly she froze – all the people on the game drive were watching her. Even worse, they were taking her picture!

“Wow,” said the guide, “this is the first time I have ever seen an aardvark! How amazing! Whoop whoop! Whoo hoo! Yay!”

“Look at her large ears that are so good at listening out for termitcs and ants! And look at that huge nose for smelling her food! And what a beautiful, enormous tail!” exclaimed the guide. “The aardvark is a remarkable animal – and it can also dig! Look at those powerful legs and claws!”

“Aardvarks are part of what we call the ‘Shy Five’,” said the guide. “This is because we very seldom see them. Look how lucky we are! This is awesome!”

Ally blushed. She didn’t realise how happy her presence made people feel – they were so excited! Ally had made their safari really special. This got her thinking: even though she looked so different, it was not a reason for her to feel shy after all.

These days, Ally is not always so shy. She is still nocturnal and she still likes to rest in her burrow during the day. But maybe, just maybe, if you look very carefully on your next safari, you might just spot Ally or one of her Shy Five friends.

Now wouldn't that be very lucky indeed!

About the Author

Combining his deep appreciation of wildlife with a calling to educate children about the responsibility of conservation, nature guide Ian Pletzer uses adorable animal characters to highlight their importance to the planet and combines these messages with small life lessons related to personal development.

Ally the Aardvark and the Shy Five is his second book.

The Safari Series is dedicated to the future conservationists of the World.

Other books in *The Safari Series*:

Henry the Hyena Loses His Giggle